Fable.

Tanya Rose Jikku

BookLeaf
Publishing

Presentation by *BookLeaf Publishing*

Web: www.bookleafpub.com

E-mail: info@bookleafpub.com

ISBN: 9789358731941

First edition 2024

*To a little girl who felt too much for her heart
and thought too much for her mind,*

this one's for you.

ACKNOWLEDGEMENT

There it is. As proud as I am of this book, it could never have come to be if I were on my own.

My Lord and Saviour, without whom I am nothing. My family, my backbone and my breath. Amma and Appa, the love you give me has formed everything I am and have. Rhea and Jiya, you guys keep me smiling and remind me to calm down. My friends, who are the only ones who can get me to stop moping. I am able to do anything that I can only with each of you by my side. And for that, I am eternally in love with you. Thank you does not cover it.

And remember, each of you human beings, that you are beautiful by every morsel that you are.
It's not over.
You have a pulse.

PREFACE

Hope and ire. Solace and verity. Bliss and bother.

Poetry is an escape. It takes you to worlds you can only wish did exist. Poetry is emptying your heart and soul out, translating dimensional embers into human language. And that's exactly what it's always been for me as I've navigated my way on this Earth. Being a person who's struggled to express myself my entire life, I found solace in script.

Feel free to indulge these poems to be whatever you want them to be. My greatest hope would be that you are able to nurture a little piece of yourself through my words.

Streams

Clouds slip
As the world turns at the pace of a snail.
In every inch
Time glazes by.

And I want to be there.
With the vapours,
Sucked in
And drowning
In the endless current of seconds.

If only my finger would graze,
then I could slice their stream
to a drought.

Leave the Light On

Leave the light on
'cause the night steals.
The night preys and suffocates.
The once peaceful hum in moist,
now blaring thrum.

Leave the light on,
because the quiet is empty.
The spaces in silence,
too naked to bear.

The gap between atoms turns too vacuum
letting 'mares intrude,
like the silence,
where they be unwanted.

The dark unveils
what the light kept secret;
by blinding the pain in every vein.

The dark rips security,
from where it was snug,
And cripples the voice that wanted hope.

Leave the light on.
For when the night comes,
I'll dread the dark.

You'll Stay

Don't try.
Try so hard to hold on.
Don't try so hard.
The leaf wants loose.

It wants to go.
It wants to embrace the wind
And drown the lake
It has always dreamed.

Don't hold on to the raindrop
On your knuckle.
So cool, so precious,
Your heart yearns to touch.

But your skin will rot.
The drop will dry.
It wants to go.

The warmth can't forever stain your sheets.
The tea runs cold on being left out.
The sunset fades in the ring of a bell.
And then the night can hug you,
Dead silence in its grout.
Where will you go then?

You'll stay.
Statue on the roof
Staring at all
But nothing at all.

And the bugs will hit your skin,
The damp will lick your ankles
And your knees will buck from standing stiff.

Yet you'll stay.
You will stay and not dare a blink.
All because you didn't think it would leave
And go away so soon
Just this one day.

the swindler.

it scorches in my lungs
cracking my ribs
my conscience gives way
as deep dark dread settles itself
in the core of my being

and i'm haunted by that
single stupid second
i was blinded by the glint in your eye
to quash the oaths
of my spirit
while you ruined everything
i was

Friday Nights

… somewhere between life and death
somewhere between
unbearable joy
and debilitating disgust

not among flashing lights
or by the beach downtown
that's where I'll be found
on a Friday night …

Gardening

If she ran,
What would you do?

Cut grass.
Clipped and shred.
Lighter green tips and earth.
Raw dirty, sludgey, red earth.

And that smell.
Tell me, what's more sound.

The mower against the wall.
You're crumpled on the ground.
Just like every other day,
You lay.

Though now, still.
You're barely breathing at all.
And today
She towers over you, tall.

Weeds in hand
And a countenance of glory.
It's about time she took over the story.

Don't you think her fury's fairness?
After all, she's dealt with you in your bareness?

So tell me.
If she ran,
What could you do?

You can't trip ankles
With a hand
Sliced off by a tool.

When Mother Mourns

Sobbing frozen pearls
Lashing trees
Howling winds
And the withering freeze

The soak reached her bone
The glaze frost her lips
She stood still
While Mother's mourn pounded skin

Though as drops slipped away
Having washed away the heat of the day
She pondered why she'd stayed
Eyes scrunched eyes were blearily opened
And there stained tears in her gaze

Till winter's breath

gentle creature
please tell me why
why you hold your breath
when the eagle comes

why your wings are clipped by your side
why your ears stick pulled
into your crown

my fingers tease
static spine
bumpy and rock
like the mounds of a wave

daggers pierce my neck
my hand is forced away
why can't i stay

if only till the trembling
stills in your joints
if only till the redness
leaves your nose

till the winter
then the brutes
are corpse
in their caves

Sink

Are the tides to turn,
When sailors call at sun's break?
Or sink with the moon?

Dosage

Line by line the words stare back
And spill along
The curves of comprehension.

They cry for my praise at their assonance;
how they challenge the stars by their
wit.

How if only
I'd let them claim my
breath.

They'd crackle my nerves like a
nameless drug.

Mr. Bluey

A little scarf snuggles my neck.
I have a little brown nose and eyes to match.
Fuzzy little ears, my dear, you'd always pull.
Now I look at your tears and my hollow eyes
turn full.

I never seem to grasp
Our bitter tale.
Only a dumpling you were,
At four, you'd hold my tail.
Dragged across the carpet as you grappled for
Mum.
On all your blocks, my head would thump.

When I was made yours you could hardly walk!
I've witnessed all your tumbles and talks.
Tussling me with grimey fingers,
I'm sure the whiff of mustard still lingers.
Just a pling, hardly 6 years old,
Your nose would wrinkle as you raved on Mrs.
Harold!

When I first saw tears,
must've been Thursday.

Seeing eyes that swam,
I was yanked up your hand.
You bawled and bawled, just holding me tight.
Whimpers that'd have pierced me, had I had life.

Those giggles and rumbles with your friends,
I'll clutch them in my heart to the very end.
For years have passed, I think can say
That, at some point, I became a stray.

Only dust for warmth;
I'm splayed on the counter.
The marble can be a little chill
In the winter.

I see you wail,
Still on your bed.
The only difference is
I'm not being held.

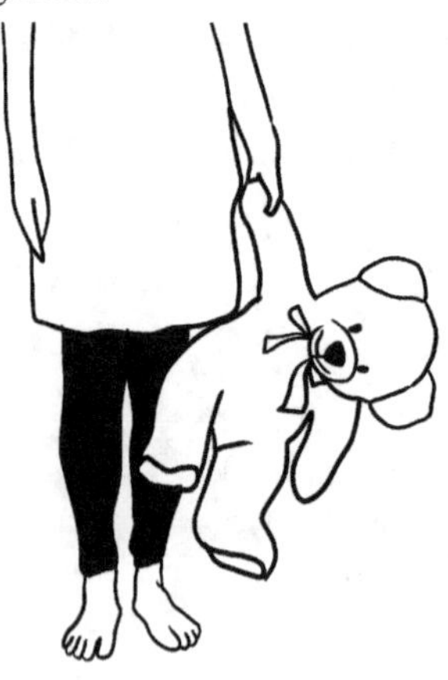

Just like Icarus

I know I'm just like Icarus
But somehow, I'm not too sure.

I remember the wings from before I could
babble;
When I'd reach Mum's gaze or
When Dad would make a face.
They fluttered always then
But I didn't mind them.

Boy, have I flown a lot since then.
Though, I do not seem to recall every flutter,
When my heart would skip
In my ribs
And I was a little warmer.

All I can remember is the feeling.
Those moments are just a blur.
But those dives,
When my wings froze stiff,
I could tell you all about them in my slumber.

Just when the wind slaps your face
And you feel your insides sink.
Those screaming, silent moments

When you feel everything
But nothing at all.

It gets colder then, though.
The chill just barely skins your bones.
I've tried to fight that, naturally.
The warm blood has instincts, you know.
So off I took towards that sun.

Though, I must've flown too far.
Too close.
Higher and higher,
as I tried to escape.
Warmer and drier, my feathers scorched and
burned.

So, I've grown to like the sinking more.
However frozen I felt, so deep.
I prefer that to the scalding heat.

It's safe here, my friends.
Somewhere between the stars and dread
There is a safe place where all is well.

So though, I'm just like Icarus
I don't understand him.

Metal Bars

Let me out
Those eyes
They're too deep
Too vast too wide

They hold too much light
Too much dark
Too much of what I can't tell
Too much that's much too clear

Screaming syllables
In my face
Melt into
Gibberish glaze

Am I a prisoner,
Or a pet,
In that gaze
I can't tell
Yet.

Pity Points

With words
like a siren
And forged faiths devout,
I fell for the stutters
In your
Mellifluent meltdown.

The Great Big Tragedy

Sky blinks white.
Her tears are proud.
She carries scars
In lightning's
Lance.

Can you hear her wailing
Among the cracks?

She roars and roars
On every pierce
And we listen on
With wary leer.

You call her loud,
Obnoxious, foul.
In her calamity
You shall drown.

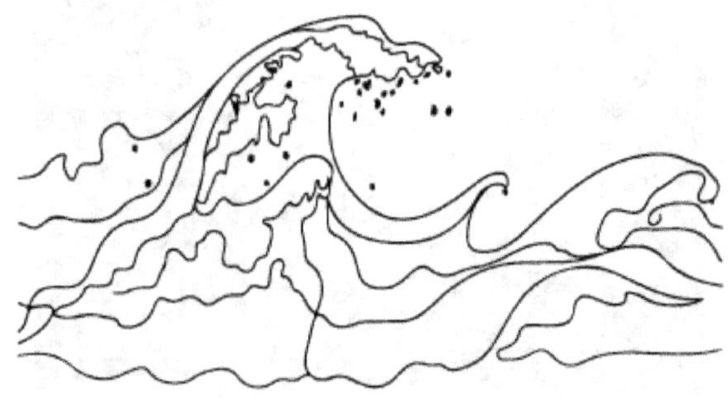

HUM

Secrets
Space
Silence

There's such glory
In these seconds
As the beats
Flow around us
And the sun
Creeps
Through every crack

Ebbing thunder
Crackling fire
Dances in the ions
Can you hear
their song?
Can't you tell they want you
Clasped
in their ripples?

Vacuum

The space between stars is
a universe of vacuum.

In every wink
we mistake,
is a desperate loom to a lover,
lucid in its ache.

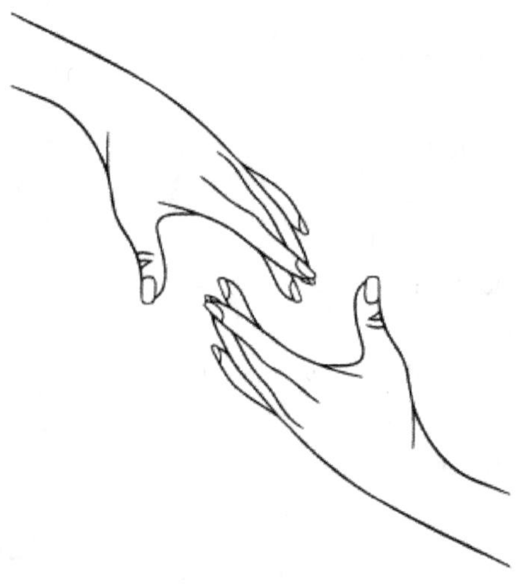

Clones

Fake fake
Facades
In faces.
Like ruse to rivet.
Hoax to hive.

We wear masks on our psyches
To cover up the shards.
I see you for a second
Then I'm shut out far.

Like a door to deck.
A wall to win.
Your eyes are a shadow in that murky thing.
The glint seems so far
But I almost see it.
Why can't you just let me hold it?

I see such a glow;
Believe me when I tell you so.
What could be wrong with your bare skin
That I can't graze
Glorious angles, cracks and dents.
Don't lie
That the mask hasn't sliced you more.

If only for a second,
I want to know
What bleeds onto the carpet
When the mask is cracked on the floor.

I've hated that thing
Since you first slid it on.
Don't tell me
That it makes you calm.

I've heard your whimpers.
When you're in front of the mirror.
When you wash your face,
The mask on the dresser.

if i could just hold you,
i promise i'll be gentle.
the copies have nothing
on your crystal.

Corrosion

graveyard mirage kicks in
don't tell me where you've been
i love you doesn't grin
tears fall
i won't hold your chin
or look you in the eyes as you break

i won't see
the rusty fractals
in that lake

Parallels

All humans
  really
    are the same.

All we do
is tolerate.

Because
in this fickle fib
  really
    we're not the same
at all.

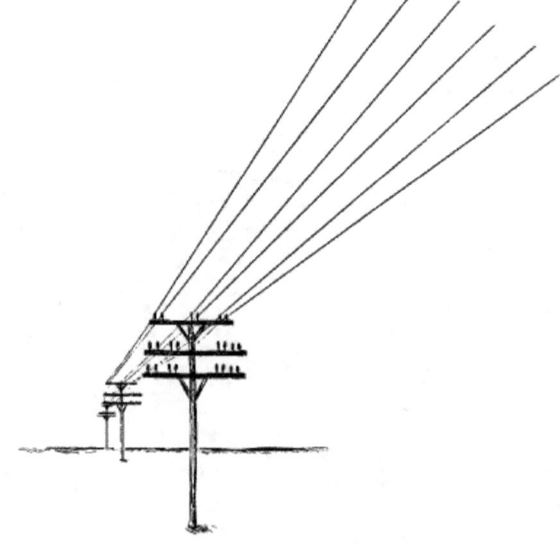

Two Words

Thank you.
Two simple words that almost don't belong…

Yet slip off my tongue so easy
As my gaze falls on 6 pm sky.
Each wisp, each hue flicked at absolute
perfection;
It doesn't seem real.
It's not like yesterday's.

When breath from the heavens kisses my face,
My hair, set free,
But my skin's ablaze.
It takes my soul's wear with it
And once more, there's warmth I cannot limit.

When my heart is so full
My fingers tremble.
My knees go weak.
I look into those eyes and two words are much
too simple
For such a miracle.

There is a haven so sound.
Where laughter rings in the walls

And memories hug in every corner.
How the scent of home
Can make me wonder;

How two simple words have so much meaning.
How the sun rises every morning.
Without fail, that alarm goes off
And I feel cool breeze
Touch my lungs.

Be it sun or moon
Or earth or star,
You reign over them all.
And each moment, you must awe
At how two simple words
Can mean such a roar.

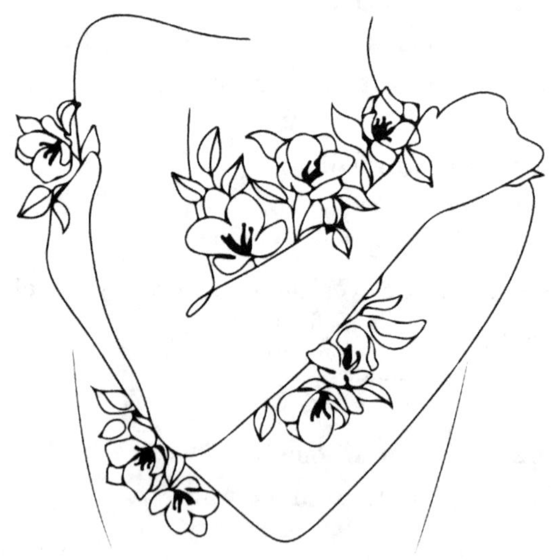

Wordery

In a world
Where babble drains
Like spears
To the psyche

Your words wet my soul.

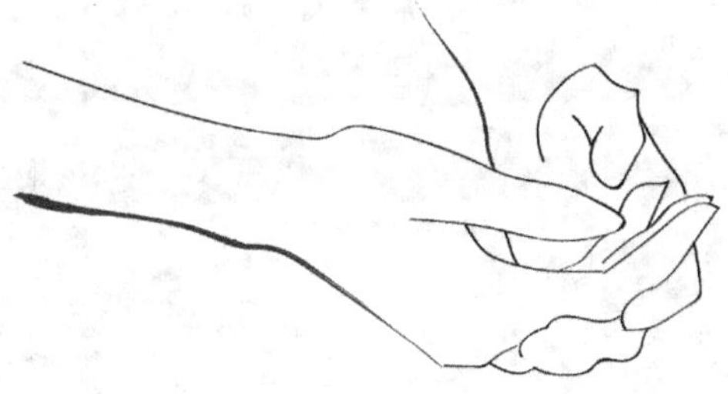

Reading

I'm an open book
But no one's ever liked reading.

I've sung melodies
but their ears were plugged.

I've built skyscrapers with precision.

But the sun's stroke
Sears skin through crystal.

Cold

Your chest doesn't rise again
I can never see you smile again
You will never hold my hand again

So my lips close your eyelids
Gone cold
How can I live in a world without you?

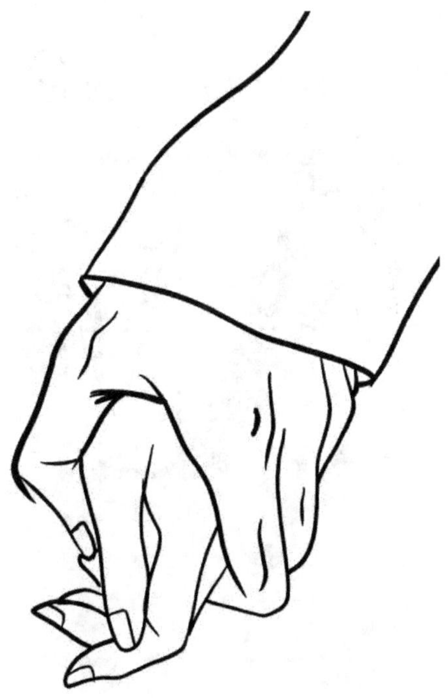

Nuzzle

It is the most ludicrous feeling to feel yourself
falling in love;

Awful enough to keep you awake,
Lull enough to nuzzle sleep.

Ruins

35

The only remains
Of what it did
Was purple's kiss
On her lower eyelid.

Isn't it funny

Isn't it funny
That the ones for whom
Our hearts
Beat
Are also the ones
For whom
She bleeds.

Birthday Girl

i blow out the candles.
it's just another day.

as the tears dried on my cheeks
i asked
why we don't celebrate the bad days
instead of birthdays
if older is what i've become.

Pulse

Two fingers, my love.
Right at the crevice of your
throat.
There you go.
Do you feel it?
A gentle thrum?
So faint it's barely there?
A fool would miss it,
But you feel it, don't you?

The lilac caress on your fingers,
Like a mother's song.
It's real, my love.
A palpable yet inscrutable
Piece of evidence
That the crook's gotten nowhere near
your heart.

You're alright.
The pulse
Is strong.

9 789358 731941